my *Florida* garden

a gardener's journal

Tom MacCubbin

COOL
SPRINGS
PRESS

NOTE: The ideas expressed in this book are not, in all cases, exact quotations, as some have been edited to fit the format. In all cases, the publisher has attempted to maintain the speaker's original intent. Further, in some cases, source materials for this book were obtained from secondary sources, primarily print media and the Internet. While every effort has been made to ensure the accuracy of these sources, accuracy cannot be guaranteed. To notify us of any corrections or clarifications, please contact Cool Springs Press.

Cool Springs Press, Inc.
112 Second Avenue North
Franklin, TN 37064

First Printing 2000
Printed in the United States of America
10 9 8 7 6 5 4 3 2 1

Design by: Sheri Ferguson
Illustrations by: Allison Starcher
Editorial Consultant: Erica Glasener

Visit the Cool Springs Press website at www.coolspringspress.com

my *Florida* garden

a gardener's journal

this is my

Florida

garden

_____
name

_____
year

why keep a garden journal ?

Welcome! We Florida gardeners know that to garden in this state is an exciting and unexpected mix of contrasts. We also know there are many elements to balance in order to garden successfully. That's why you will appreciate *My Florida Garden: A Gardener's Journal.*

Keeping a garden journal will help you keep track of how your garden grows. You will discover which plants thrive, which ones struggle, and best of all, you will discover many surprises. More than just record keeping, journaling is a way to trace your growth as a gardener. Writing down your favorite moments in the garden may help you decide which plants to add or which ones to replace. How does your garden make you feel? You may discover you prefer one season to another. Maybe your style of gardening has changed. A journal will help you track the evolution in your garden.

As gardeners know, weather is a huge factor in plant performance. By keeping track of air temperature, the amount of rainfall, and drastic changes (storms or droughts), we can see which plants survived and plan better for next year.

Has the environment in your garden changed? Trees and shrubs that were once small may have matured and created a shadier garden. Keeping a list of what you plant, where and when you plant it, and the source of the plant will provide useful information for the future.

Further, keeping up with what's blooming when, and how long it blooms is another reason to take time to write daily or weekly in a garden journal. You might be surprised at how many seasons your garden features beautiful blooms, colorful foliage, or fantastic fruits. Some of the best color combinations happen by accident and remembering which plant blooms and when it blooms from year to year is not easy. But with good journal records you may recreate pleasing plant combinations and avoid repeating mistakes.

How often you fertilize, prune, and water are other things to keep track of in your garden journal. Which techniques have been most successful? If you have a particular pest or disease problem with one plant, what methods were effective in eradicating or controlling the problem? If your roses were beautiful last year, when did you prune them and how much did you prune? When did you divide your daylilies and where did you plant the different varieties of spring bulbs? All of these questions can be answered in the pages of *My Florida Garden*.

getting started with your garden journal

By keeping daily records, you can check your journal and chart your most successful garden practices. Whether it's how and when you propagated a favorite hydrangea or rose, when the first hibiscus came into bloom, or when you first noticed the scent of a particular native azalea, your Florida garden journal will provide the ideal format for keeping in touch with your garden and what it can teach you. Here's how to get started.

- Designate a day and a time during the week to write in your journal. You might discover that early morning coffee time or the end of the day works best.

- Use a favorite pen and keep it with your journal. Write brief, clear notes (*rainy and cool with temp around 60° F, cannas have been in bloom for 2 weeks, rose bush loaded with flower buds, planted two shell gingers*).

- Keep a 5" x 7" envelope tucked in the back of your journal to hold photographs and pictures from catalogues or magazines that inspire you. Be sure to identify and label pictures.

- List existing trees, shrubs, perennials, and bulbs including a sketch of where they are located. This will be especially helpful over the years when you make changes in your garden.

   Once you get used to journaling, you may find that you look forward to writing about your garden as much as you enjoy adding new plants.

To create a beautiful Florida garden, think about what you want your garden to do, how you want to use it, how it might fit into your life, and how much of your life you want to fit into it. Soil, climate, and microclimates (small pockets within a zone that have warmer or colder temperatures, depending upon geography) are the parameters within which you will work. Begin by finding your location on the hardiness zone map. The most recent map divides the state into areas with the same annual minimum temperatures, from zones 8 through 11. Zones 8, 9, and 10 are subdivided into zone 8A, zone 8B, zone 9A, zone 9B, zone 10A, and zone 10B. A small wedge of North Florida, in zone 8A, has minimum winter temperatures of 10° to 15° F, while zone 11 in the Florida Keys has minimum winter temperatures above 40° F. Most of the state is subtropical, while North Florida is similar to Texas, Louisiana, and Georgia.

Study the environmental conditions in your garden and let the garden tell you what to do. Familiarize yourself with the native or common plants of your region and use them as a guide to selections for your garden — both native and exotic. Knowing the type of soil, light, and exposure your plants require will help you select the right plant for the right place. With the exception of large trees and shrubs, don't be afraid to move your plants. Often conditions change, and what was once a favorable environment may no longer be. Proper watering, mulch, and fertilizer further help to ensure the success of your garden.

the plan

It is often useful to consult a professional garden designer or landscape architect to help you plan your garden. Their work can be as detailed as a drawing with every plant sited or as broad as a simple list of recommended plants for particular areas. If you have just moved into your house, observe the garden one whole growing season before you hire someone to help you develop a plan. This experience will help you determine which areas receive the most light and which are in shade, etc. Once you have a plan, you can implement it in stages over time. Making adjustments as conditions or your tastes change is easy. You may also want to refer to my book *Florida Gardener's Guide* (Cool Springs Press, 1997) for specific plant recommendations and advice for Florida gardeners.

soil

Good soil is essential for a fruitful garden but few Floridians are blessed with perfect soil. Good soil is rich in organic matter and holds moisture, but is also well drained. Most plants prosper in slightly acid to neutral soils although there is a long list of plants, native and exotic, that will tolerate high pH (alkaline) soils. The alkalinity may cause leaf yellowing from magnesium, manganese, or iron deficiency, however. In both sandy and rocky soils, certain mineral elements will leach away in heavy rains. Sandy and rocky soils both require irrigation, while limestone will hold water longer in little niches and crevices. It is important to know what type of soil you have in order to garden successfully.

amending your soil

Compost is one of the best soil amendments because it is alive with billions of creatures to help roots absorb water and nutrients. Decomposed leaves, lawn clippings, pruned branches, and discarded plant parts harbor the beneficial fungi, bacteria, and other living creatures that are important parts of healthy soil.

Making compost can be as simple as piling leaves and clippings in a heap and letting them break down. You can add kitchen waste such as coffee grounds, clean eggshells, and uncooked vegetable scraps to your compost pile. It is best not to add animal fats, bones, or meat. Be patient! It will take approximately six months and a 30-gallon bag of yard trimmings to yield 1 cubic foot of compost from your pile.

Ground pine bark is a common soil amendment found throughout the state. Gardeners can also use ground peanut hulls. Although peat moss is readily available, it breaks down too quickly. The best organic matter is found in manure, compost, and other materials.

You may spread a 2-inch layer of this amendment over a flowerbed and then mix it with the soil underneath. You will need 2 cubic feet of soil conditioner (store-bought or homemade compost) for every 8 square feet of flowerbed. For best results, mix organic matter into a depth of 6-8 inches. Work the soil when it is dry to avoid clods forming when the soil becomes wet. You will also get a more even mixture.

watering

Watering seems like a simple thing, but gardeners have a tendency to overwater or underwater plants. Sandy soils drain quickly, requiring watering at least twice a week during blistering summers. Clay soils hold water; therefore, plants growing in clay need less watering.

guidelines for watering:

- Water your container plants until the water runs out the bottom. During our rainy summer months some containers may not need additionl water. Do not water until the top inch of the soil is dry to the touch.
- Put a hose at the base of a newly installed tree or shrub and thoroughly soak the root ball daily for several weeks. As the plant grows, the area that needs to be soaked will increase as the root zone increases.
- Use shallow cans (tuna, etc.) to measure the amount of water applied by your lawn sprinkler. Put six cans in the area you are watering and run the system for an hour. Then measure the depth of the water in all cans. When the average depth of the water is $1/2$ inch, the grass root zone has been irrigated. This may take 45 minutes to an hour.

- Buy an inexpensive water timer and a few soaker hoses. They are a worthwhile investment. During periods of drought mature trees will benefit from long, slow watering.

mulch

Mulch acts like a blanket, holding moisture in the soil and keeping the soil temperature from getting too hold or too cold. Mulch can also help control weed infestations.

tips when mulching:
- Apply a 1- to 2-inch layer of mulch on top of the soil around all plants. At the same time avoid piling mulch against the trunks or stems of plants. This could lead to potential disease problems.
- Wood chips, shredded leaves, pecan hulls, and coco hulls are good choices.

nutrients

The main nutrients plants need are nitrogen, phosphorous, and potassium. When you buy fertilizer you will see three numbers on the bag representing the percentage of each nutrient in the mixture. For example, a bag of 10-10-10 fertilizer contains 10% nitrogen (N), 10% phosphorus (P), and 10% potassium (K). The other 70% is inert filler such as clay or sand.

Each nutrient serves a function in the overall good health of a plant. Nitrogen promotes leaf growth. That is why lawn fertilizer has a high nitrogen percentage. Phosphorous is important in the formation of roots as well as flower, seed, and fruit growth. That is why starter fertilizers and bloom fertilizers have high percentages of phosphorous. Potassium increases overall cell health. When plants are under stress from drought or cold, adequate potassium helps the plant withstand the crisis.

soil test

A soil test helps determine how much fertilizer to apply and whether additives (such as lime) are needed. You can purchase a kit to test your soil or have it done through the University of Florida's Cooperative Extension Service. Every county has an Extension office, and the phone number is under the individual county listings in the phone directory. They will give you a written report describing the nutrients present in the soil, the amounts in which they are present, and specific recommendations for the amounts of fertilizer and any additives needed.

Soil acidity is measured in numbers from 1 to 14 on the pH scale. Most plants prefer a soil that has a pH of 6.0 to 6.5. It takes a lot of lime to move the pH up to 6.5. Your soil test will determine the pH of your soil and what, if anything, should be done to protect it.

get started journaling and have fun

Your garden is what you make it. If you keep your heart and mind open to the nuances of nature, you will cultivate more than just pretty flowers and strong trees. Both you and your plants will grow in your beautiful garden. Hopefully, you will also have fun creating lovely gardens. May you have all the sun and rain you need!

Florida Garden Favorites

I selected a list of plants that are easy to grow, readily available, adaptable to various growing conditions, and help provide year-round interest. These plants can be very beneficial to your Florida garden because they provide brilliant color, some attract birds and wildlife, and most require minimal maintenance. You will find all of my recommendations in my book, co-authored with Georgia Tasker, *Florida Gardener's Guide* (Cool Springs Press. 1997). Give these a try!

Annuals

- Impatiens — *Impatiens wallerana*
- Coleus — *Coleus* x *hybridus*
- Geranium — *Pelargonium hortorum*
- Torenia — *Torenia fournieri*
- Marigold — *Tagetes patula*
- Pansy — *Viola* x *wittrockiana*
- Petunia — *Petunia* x *hybrida*
- Salvia — *Salvia* spp.
- Dianthus — *Dianthus* x *hybrida*
- Dusty Miller — *Senecio cineraria*

Bulbs

- Caladium — *Caladium* x *hortulanum*
- Amaryllis — *Hippeastrum* hybrids
- African Iris — *Dietes bicolor*
- Day Lily — *Hemerocallis* hybrids
- Gladiolus — *Gladiolus* hybrids
- Zephyr Lily — *Zephyranthes* spp.
- Blood Lily — *Haemanthus multiflorus*
- Canna — *Canna* hybrids
- Shell Ginger — *Alpinia zerumbet*
- Louisiana Iris — *Iris* hybrids

Groundcovers

- Small Leaf Confederate Jasmine — *Trachelospermum asiaticum*
- Liriope — *Liriope muscari*
- Mexican Heather — *Cuphea hyssopifolia*
- Wedelia — *Wedelia trilobata*
- Blue Daze — *Evolvulus glomeratus*
- English Ivy — *Hedera helix*
- Cast Iron Plant — *Aspidistra elatior*
- Mondo Grass — *Ophiopogon japonicus*
- Shore Juniper — *Juniperus conferta*
- Broad Sword Fern — *Nephrolepis biserrata*

Orchids

- Cattleyas — *Cattleya* spp.
- Oncidium — *Oncidium* spp.
- Phalaenopsis — *Phalaenopsis* spp.
- Vanda — *Vanda* spp.
- Dendrobiums — *Dendrobium* spp.
- Epidendrum — *Epidendrum* spp.
- Paphiopedilum — *Paphiopedilum* spp.

Ornamental Grasses

- Fountain Grass — *Pennisetum setaceum*
- Muhly Grass — *Muhlenbergia capellaris*
- Pampas Grass — *Cortaderia selloana*
- Sand Cordgrass — *Spartina bakeri*
- Wiregrass — *Aristida beyrichiana*
- Purple Lovegrass — *Eragrostis spectablis*
- Lopsided Indiangrass — *Sorghastrum secundum*
- Florida Gamma Grass — *Tripsacum floridana*

Palms

- Cabbage Palm — *Sabal palmetto*
- Butia Palm — *Butia capitata*
- Chinese Fan Palm — *Livistona chinesis*
- Lady Palm — *Rhapis* spp.
- Pygmy Date Palm — *Phoenix roebelenii*
- Royal Palm — *Roystonea elata*
- Saw Palmetto — *Serenoa repens*
- Coconut Palm — *Cocos nucifera*

Perennials

- Pentas — *Pentas lanceolata*
- Salvia — *Salvia* spp.
- Begonia — *Begonia* spp.
- Bird-of-Paradise — *Strelitzia reginae*
- Periwinkle — *Catharanthus roseus*
- Society Garlic — *Tulbaghia violacea*
- Wild Petunia — *Ruellia caroliniensis*
- Leather Fern — *Acrostichum danaeifolium*
- Asparagus Fern — *Asparagus setaceus*

Roses

- Hybrid Tea Rose — *Rosa* hybrids
- Grandiflora Rose — *Rosa* hybrids
- Floribunda — *Rosa* hybrids
- Miniature Rose — *Rosa* hybrids
- Old Garden Rose — *Rosa* hybrids
- Climbing Rose — *Rosa* hybrids

Shrubs

- Crape Myrtle — *Laegerstromia indica*
- Hibiscus — *Hibiscus rosa-sinensis*
- Ligustrum — *Ligustrum japonicum*
- Ixora — *Ixora coccinea*
- Croton — *Codiaeum variegatum*
- Gardenia — *Gardenia jasminoides*
- Azalea — *Rhododendron* spp.
- Oleander — *Nerium oleander*

Trees

- Crape Myrtle — *Lagerstroemia indica*
- Tabebuia — *Tabebuia impetiginosa*
- Bottlebrush — *Callistemon rigidus*
- Live Oak — *Quercus virginiana*
- Sweet Gum — *Liquidambar styraciflua*
- Sweetbay — *Magnolia virginiana*
- Orange Tree — *Citrus sinensis*
- Geiger Tree — *Cordia sebestena*

Tropical plants

- Bromeliad — *Aechmea*
- Ginger — *Alpinia* spp.
- Heliconias — *Heliconia* spp.
- Anthurium — *Anthurium* spp.
- Philodendron — *Philodendron* spp.
- Peace Lily — *Spathiphyllum* spp.
- Fern — *Adiantum* spp.
- Ti Plant — *Cordyline terminalis*

Turfgrasses

- St. Augustinegrass — *Stenotaphrum secundatum*
- Bahiagrass — *Paspalum notatum*
- Bermudagrass — *Cynodon species*
- Zoysiagrass — *Zoysia species*
- Centipedegrass — *Eremochloa ophiuroides*

Vines

- Confederate Jasmine — *Trachelospermum jasminoides*
- Bougainvillea — *Bougainvillea* spp.
- Flame Vine — *Pyrostegia venusta*
- Coral Honeysuckle — *Lonicera sempervirens*
- Passion Vine — *Passiflora* spp.
- Carolina Yellow Jasmine — *Gelsemium sempervirens*
- Wisteria — *Wisteria sinensis*
- Trumpet Creeper — *Campsis radicans*

Cycads

- All Varieties

{ f l o r i d a   h a r d i n e s s   z o n e   m a p }

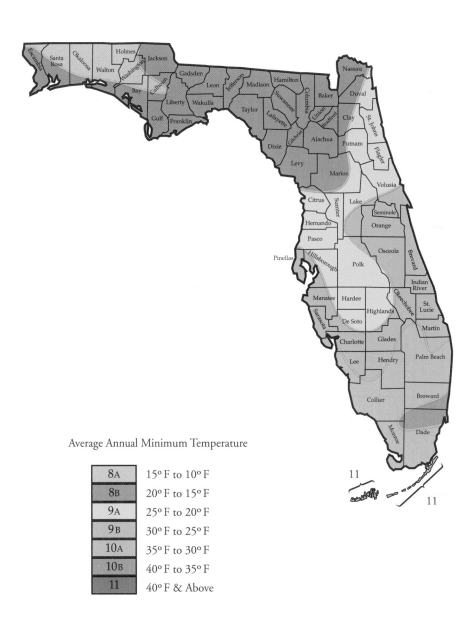

Average Annual Minimum Temperature

8A	15° F to 10° F
8B	20° F to 15° F
9A	25° F to 20° F
9B	30° F to 25° F
10A	35° F to 30° F
10B	40° F to 35° F
11	40° F & Above

To create a
little flower is the
labour of ages.

— *William Blake*

january | week 1

January

garden observations

_____
_____
_____
_____
_____
_____

what's the weather like?

_____
_____
_____
_____
_____

Start the year off right! Photograph your garden at least once every month. This will help you with your planning and planting schemes.

what have I planted/transplanted?

_____
_____
_____
_____

garden notes

What is a weed? A
plant whose virtues have
not yet been dicovered.

—Ralph Waldo Emerson

January

garden observations

Order seeds now for your favorite annuals, perennials and vegetables. Cut out color photographs and create your own record for what you order.

what's the weather like?

When planning your garden, use a large sheet of graph paper with 1/4 inch grids. A scale of 1 inch = 4 feet is a useful proportion.

what have I planted/transplanted?

garden notes

January

garden observations

_____

_____

_____

_____

_____

_____

what's the weather like?

_____

_____

_____

what have I planted/transplanted?

_____

_____

_____

_____

_____

_____

garden notes

Check house plants for signs of insects and disease. Spots, speckles or webs on leaves indicate pests are present.

january | week 3

January

garden observations

_____

_____

_____

_____

_____

what's the weather like?

_____

_____

_____

_____

_____

_____

Tip to Remember:
You may also use
vegetables as
ornamental plants.
Ornamental peppers
and sweet potato vine
selections are good
examples.

what have I planted/transplanted?

_____

_____

_____

_____

_____

_____

garden notes

february | week 1

February

garden observations

_____

_____

_____

_____

_____

what's the weather like?

_____

_____

_____

_____

Take a walk through your garden, and plan additions to create winter interest for next year.

what have I planted/transplanted?

_____

_____

Did You Know? The only tulip color that has not yet been developed is any shade of blue.

_____

_____

_____

garden notes

february | week 2

February

garden observations

_____

_____

_____

_____

_____

what's the weather like?

_____

_____

_____

_____

When in doubt,
call your local
Extension Service.
Master Gardeners
there will provide
information (and
the advice is free!)

what have I planted/transplanted?

_____

_____

_____

_____

garden notes

February

garden observations

Extend the life of your cut flowers. Remove the lower leaves and re-cut the stems before arranging them in lukewarm water.

what's the weather like?

what have I planted/transplanted?

garden notes

Though I do not believe
that a plant will spring
up where no seed has been,
I have great faith in a
seed. Convince me that
you have a seed there,
and I am prepared to
expect wonders.

— Henry David Thoreau

february | week 3

february | week 4

February

garden observations

_____

_____

_____

_____

_____

what's the weather like?

_____

_____

_____

_____

_____

Tip to Remember:
Fill clear plastic
milk jugs with
water and place
around young
tomato plants.
They will provide
warmth overnight
for young plants,
helping you get a
jump on spring.

what have I planted/transplanted?

_____

_____

_____

_____

_____

garden notes

february | week 4

march | week 1

March

what's blooming?

Direct sow wildflower
seeds where you want
them to grow in
climates with USDA
zones 1 through 6.
(Check the zone map
in the introduction to
identify your zone.)

what's the weather like?

Take a soil test now
so you will know how
to prepare your garden
for the next season.

what have I planted/transplanted?

garden notes

march | week 2

March

what's blooming?

Tip to Remember:
Plan to add a few
annuals to your
perennial garden
to help provide
season-long blooms.

what's the weather like?

Watch for aphids on
shrubs as they leaf out.
Treat with insecticidal
soap or any other
labeled pesticide,
if needed.

what have I planted/transplanted?

Start tomato seeds for
transplants 4-6 weeks
before optimum plant-
ing time in your area.

garden notes

march | week 2

m a r c h | w e e k 3

March

what's blooming?

Single-flower forms of
marigolds and zinnias
are more appealing to
butterflies than the
double-flower forms.

what's the weather like?

Did You Know?
Viburnum is a
member of the
honeysuckle family.

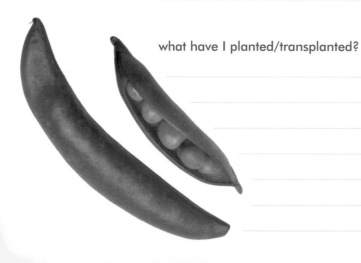

what have I planted/transplanted?

garden notes

m a r c h | w e e k 4

March

what's blooming?

what's the weather like?

Hummingbirds love
tubular flowers such
as trumpet vine, coral
honeysuckle, and
nicotiana. Plant lots
of these if you want to
attract hummingbirds.

what have I planted/transplanted?

garden notes

Half the interest of a garden is the constant exercise of the imagination.

— C.W. Earle

april week 1

what's blooming?

what's the weather like?

Have you
photographed
your garden lately?
This will help with
your garden planning
and design ideas.

what have I planted/transplanted?

An easy time to weed
is the day after a
gentle rain, when the
soil is slightly moist,
and weeds are easy to
pull—roots and all.

garden notes

april | week 2

Propagate some
of your favorite
broadleaf shrubs using
this simple layering
technique: Select a
branch that is close to
the ground. Bend the
branch so that it is in
contact with the soil.
Cover the branch
with soil. Water well
and hold the branch
in place with a brick.
In six weeks, check to
see if there are roots.
Once the roots are
firmly established,
cut the new plant
off from the
mother plant.

what's blooming?

what's the weather like?

what have I planted/transplanted?

garden notes

As is the gardener, such is the garden.

— Hebrew Proverb

april | week 3

Tip to Remember:
When digging a hole
for a tree, it's best to
dig the hole at least
half again as wide as
the size of the rootball
(much wider is even
better). Use the same
soil you dug out to
backfill around
the rootball and
water-in well.

Turn your compost
pile. If you haven't
started one already,
call your Extension
Service for advice.

what's blooming?

what's the weather like?

what have I planted/transplanted?

april | week 4

what's the weather like?

Wooden clothespins
can be used as plant
markers.

Place grow-thru stakes
above plants that need
support in early
spring, and in a
short time they will
cover the stakes.

what have I planted/transplanted?

Plan to prune back spring-blooming azaleas and other shrubs such as forsythia or spirea after they finish flowering. This way you won't cut off any potential flower buds for next year.

Check plants once or twice a week for insect and disease problems. It's easier to control a small infestation if it's discovered early.

what's blooming?

what's the weather like?

what have I planted/transplanted?

garden notes

May

what's blooming?

_____

_____

_____

_____

_____

_____

what's the weather like?

_____

_____

_____

_____

_____

_____

Incorporate a slow-release fertilizer in the soil of hanging baskets and container plantings. This will provide nutrients for several months in one application.

what have I planted/transplanted?

_____

_____

_____

_____

_____

garden notes

Many diseases can be controlled with sanitation. Remove and destroy any infected leaves as soon as they are found.

May

what's blooming?

Parsley and fennel
provide food for
butterfly caterpillars.

what's the weather like?

Interest children
in gardening by
planning a small
child's garden. A
bean tee-pee is fun
to plant and grow!

what have I planted/transplanted?

garden notes

The best time
for slug hunting
is at night using
a flashlight and
a pair of gloves.

may | week 3

may week 4

May

what's blooming?

_____

_____

_____

_____

_____

Did You Know?
Bees are our most
efficient pollinators
for flowers, fruits,
and vegetables. Any
garden with lots of
bees is a healthy
environment.

what's the weather like?

_____

_____

_____

_____

_____

what have I planted/transplanted?

_____

_____

_____

_____

garden notes

*Tickle it with a hoe
and it will laugh
into a harvest.*

—English Proverb

June

A perennial garden looks wonderful when planted against a background of a wall, a hedge, or evergreen shrubs.

A plant's scientific name consists of a genus and an epithet. The genus and the epithet are always italicized and the genus begins with a capital letter. A third word in the name may refer to a specific variety, called a cultivar. It is set off by single quotation marks.

what's blooming?

what's the weather like?

what have I planted/transplanted?

garden notes

june week 2

what's blooming?

Use vines to create vertical interest in the garden. If you don't have a wall or fence on which to train them, a lattice or arbor will work.

what's the weather like?

You can create your own portable seep irrigation system by punching a few holes in plastic containers and placing them beside plants that need additional moisture.

what have I planted/transplanted?

garden notes

Though an old man,
I am but a young
gardener...

— Thomas Jefferson

june week 3

June

Plan to shear fall-blooming asters to make them bushier and more compact.

what's blooming?

what's the weather like?

Did You Know?
Even though a plant may be identified as self-cleaning, flowers are better off if you deadhead, or remove the spent blooms as often as you can. This will allow the plant to use its energy to make more flowers and leaves instead of making seeds.

what have I planted/transplanted?

garden notes

june | week 4

June

what's blooming?

what's the weather like?

BTK (*Bacillus thuringiensis kurstaki*) is an organic biological control that is effective against many caterpillars and is safe to use on vegetable crops. *Bacillus thuringiensis* 'San Diego' is effective against some leafeating beetles.

what have I planted/transplanted?

garden notes

july week 1

Harvest herbs for drying as soon as they come into flower. Bundle them up with a rubber band and hang them on a line in a dark, dry place with good air circulation. To preserve the best flavor once they are dry, store the herbs in airtight containers away from heat and light.

Press some flowers and add to this journal. It's a pretty record of what you planted.

what's blooming?

what's the weather like?

what have I planted/transplanted?

garden notes

july week 2

July

what's blooming?

_____

_____

_____

_____

_____

_____

what's the weather like?

_____

_____

_____

_____

what have I planted/transplanted?

Deadhead hybrid tea roses throughout the summer to encourage more blooms.

_____

_____

_____

_____

_____

_____

garden notes

july | week 2

july week 3

July

what's blooming?

what's the weather like?

Most unwanted
summer heat comes
through east- and west-
facing windows, not
through well-insulated
roofs and walls. Plant a
deciduous tree for shade.

what have I planted/transplanted?

garden notes

july week 4

Plants use calcium to build strong cell walls and stems. Deficiencies can cause blossom-end rot on tomatoes.

Did You Know? The Greeks and Romans used lavender in bath water. In fact, the Latin name "lavare" means, "wash".

Tip to Remember: When planting seeds, position them in geometric patterns so that you will be able to distinguish them more easily from weed seedlings.

what's blooming?

what's the weather like?

what have I planted/transplanted?

garden notes

Gardening is the purest
of human pleasures.

— Francis Bacon

august | week 1

August

what's blooming?

_____

_____

_____

_____

_____

what's the weather like?

_____

_____

_____

_____

Preserve basil leaves by mixing them in the blender with a small amount of water. Fill ice cube trays with the mixture. Once they freeze, put them in freezer bags. This way you will have basil to use in your favorite Italian dishes all winter long.

what have I planted/transplanted?

_____

_____

_____

_____

garden notes

august week 2

what's blooming?

For the best
selection, order your
spring-flowering bulbs
or purchase them
locally when they
become available in
your area. Keep them
cool and dry until
you plant them.

what's the weather like?

Take some
photographs of
your garden to refer
to later when plan-
ning for next year.

what have I planted/transplanted?

garden notes

If you haven't already done so, draw a plan of your property showing existing trees and shrubs in relation to your house. Make notes throughout the year indicating those areas that receive full sun, shade or a mix of sun and shade. This will help you to choose the right plant for the right place.

what's blooming?

what's the weather like?

what have I planted/transplanted?

august | week 4

August

what's blooming?

Water your compost
pile when the weather
has been dry.

what's the weather like?

Order three or four
types of paperwhite
narcissus to force at
two-week intervals.
You will have flowers
from Halloween into
the New Year!

what have I planted/transplanted?

Continue to harvest
vegetables as soon as
they are ripe. Regular
harvesting increases
production.

garden notes

He who plants a garden plants happiness.

—Chinese Proverb

september

what's blooming?

what's the weather like?

Expand your plant
collection by exchang-
ing seeds and plants
with fellow gardeners.

what have I planted/transplanted?

Add some shrubs to
your garden that will
offer winter interest
such as colorful bark,
or unusual shapes.

garden notes

september

what's blooming?

what's the weather like?

If you haven't
started one
already, begin
a compost pile
and let it
overwinter.
In six months
you should
have "black
gold" to mix
into your
garden.

what have I planted/transplanted?

garden notes

The frost hurts not weeds.

—Thomas Fuller

what's blooming?

what's the weather like?

what have I planted/transplanted?

If your annuals are beginning to look ragged, pull them and replace with some mums, pansies, or flowering kale.

september

Use dried seed heads such as sedum and lotus for fall decorations.

Visit your favorite nursery to select a tree or shrub for that spot in the garden that needs something new.

what's blooming?

what's the weather like?

what have I planted/transplanted?

garden notes

october | week 1

what's blooming?

what's the weather like?

Plant a tree in honor
of a birth or in
memory of a
loved one.

Fall leaf color is trig-
gered by cooler tem-
peratures, shorter
days, and less light.

what have I planted/transplanted?

garden notes

October

what's blooming?

what's the weather like?

what have I planted/transplanted?

garden notes

Sprinkle annual rye grass seed on top of the soil of pots you are forcing. By the time the bulbs bloom, it will create a green carpet underneath them.

october | week 2

what's blooming?

what's the weather like?

Tip to Remember:
Parsley is a good
plant for bed edges.
It also looks great
grown in containers
with pansies.

what have I planted/transplanted?

Use golf tees to mark
areas where bulbs are
planted.

garden notes

*Heaven is under our feet
as well as over our heads.*

—Henry David Thoreau

october

what's blooming?

what's the weather like?

Did You Know?
The word 'wort',
as in St. John's Wort,
is an old English
term that means
"medicinal plant".

what have I planted/transplanted?

garden notes

november week 1

November

what's blooming?

what's the weather like?

Fall is the best time
to direct sow wild-
flower seeds in
USDA zones 7-9.
(Check the map in
the introduction to
verify your zone.)

what have I planted/transplanted?

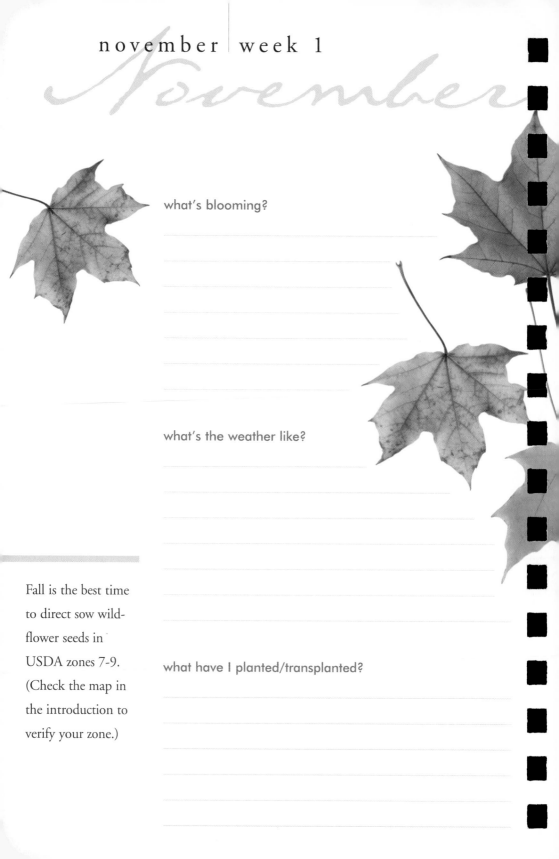

garden notes

Autumn is a second spring when every leaf is a flower. —Albert Camus

November

what's blooming?

what's the weather like?

Continue to mow
your lawn for as long
as it keeps growing.

Clean and sharpen
garden tools. Lightly
coat with oil to
prevent rust.

what have I planted/transplanted?

garden notes

what's blooming?

what's the weather like?

what have I planted/transplanted?

garden notes

Extend the life of your fresh-cut holiday tree by storing it in a cool shady place until you move it indoors. Re-cut the trunk before moving it indoors and use plenty of fresh water in the reservoir.

november | week 3

november | week 4

November

what's blooming?

For best results, store
unused seeds in a
cool, dark place in
an air- and water-
resistant container.

what's the weather like?

Selecting the right
tool for the job can
prevent most injuries.
Wear safety gear
when operating
power equipment.

what have I planted/transplanted?

garden notes

november | week 4

december | week 1

December

garden observations

_____

_____

_____

_____

_____

Make a wreath for
the holidays. Rose
hips, bittersweet, and
euonymus are good
choices for materials.

what's the weather like?

_____

_____

_____

what have I planted/
transplanted?

_____

_____

_____

_____

garden notes

*A garden is a friend
you can visit any time.*
—unknown

december | week 2

December

garden observations

_____
_____
_____
_____
_____
_____
_____

Cast iron plant,
Chinese evergreen,
heartleaf philoden-
dron, and snake plant
will tolerate low-light
conditions.

what's the weather like?

_____
_____
_____
_____
_____
_____

Tip to Remember:
The winter sun
provides the most
solar heat through
south-facing
windows. Avoid
planting shade trees
or evergreens that
may shade these
heat-absorbing
windows if you
need the extra
warmth.

what have I planted/transplanted?

_____
_____
_____
_____
_____

garden notes

december | week 3

December

garden observations

_____

_____

_____

_____

Recycle your holiday
tree. The branches
can be removed and
used as mulch. Or
you can leave the
tree intact and use it
as a windbreak and
shelter for birds.

what's the weather like?

_____

_____

_____

_____

Don't put wood
ashes in your com-
post pile; they will
alter the pH level
too much.

what have I planted/transplanted?

_____

_____

_____

_____

garden notes

December

garden observations

what's the weather like?

what have I planted/transplanted?

garden notes

Pruning large trees,
especially those located
near utilities should
be performed by a
professional. Call a
certified arborist if you
need trees pruned.

plant inventory/history

name	name
when planted	when planted
where planted	where planted
size	size
source	source
price	price

name	name
when planted	when planted
where planted	where planted
size	size
source	source
price	price

name	name
when planted	when planted
where planted	where planted
size	size
source	source
price	price

name	name
when planted	when planted
where planted	where planted
size	size
source	source
price	price

name

when planted

where planted

size

source

price

name

when planted

where planted

size

source

price

name

when planted

where planted

size

source

price

name

when planted

where planted

size

source

price

name

when planted

where planted

size

source

price

name

when planted

where planted

size

source

price

name

when planted

where planted

size

source

price

name

when planted

where planted

size

source

price

plant inventory/history

name

when planted

where planted

size

source

price

name

when planted

where planted

size

source

price

name

when planted

where planted

size

source

price

name

when planted

where planted

size

source

price

name

when planted

where planted

size

source

price

name

when planted

where planted

size

source

price

name

when planted

where planted

size

source

price

name

when planted

where planted

size

source

price

name

when planted

where planted

size

source

price

name

when planted

where planted

size

source

price

name

when planted

where planted

size

source

price

name

when planted

where planted

size

source

price

name

when planted

where planted

size

source

price

name

when planted

where planted

size

source

price

name

when planted

where planted

size

source

price

name

when planted

where planted

size

source

price

plant inventory/history

name

when planted

where planted

size

source

price

---

name

when planted

where planted

size

source

price

---

name

when planted

where planted

size

source

price

---

name

when planted

where planted

size

source

price

---

name

when planted

where planted

size

source

price

---

name

when planted

where planted

size

source

price

---

name

when planted

where planted

size

source

price

---

name

when planted

where planted

size

source

price

name

when planted

where planted

size

source

price

name

when planted

where planted

size

source

price

name

when planted

where planted

size

source

price

name

when planted

where planted

size

source

price

name

when planted

where planted

size

source

price

name

when planted

where planted

size

source

price

name

when planted

where planted

size

source

price

name

when planted

where planted

size

source

price

plant inventory/history

name

when planted

where planted

size

source

price

name

when planted

where planted

size

source

price

name

when planted

where planted

size

source

price

name

when planted

where planted

size

source

price

name

when planted

where planted

size

source

price

name

when planted

where planted

size

source

price

name

when planted

where planted

size

source

price

name

when planted

where planted

size

source

price

name

when planted

where planted

size

source

price

name

when planted

where planted

size

source

price

name

when planted

where planted

size

source

price

name

when planted

where planted

size

source

price

name

when planted

where planted

size

source

price

name

when planted

where planted

size

source

price

name

when planted

where planted

size

source

price

name

when planted

where planted

size

source

price

my garden plan

suppliers & resources

photos